T0355839

Also by Katie Peterson

This One Tree

Permission

The Accounts

A Piece of Good News

Life in a Field

AS EDITOR

New Selected Poems,

by Robert Lowell

FOG AND SMOKE

KATIE

PETERSON

FOG

AND

SMOKE

FARRAR

STRAUS

GIROUX

NEW

YORK

—

Farrar, Straus and Giroux
120 Broadway, New York 10271

Printed in the United States of America
Published in 2024 by Farrar, Straus and Giroux
First paperback edition, 2025

The Library of Congress has cataloged the hardcover edition as follows:
Names: Peterson, Katie, 1974– author.
Title: Fog and smoke : poems / Katie Peterson.
Description: First edition. | New York : Farrar, Straus and Giroux, 2024. |
Identifiers: LCCN 2023031243 | ISBN 9780374610890 (hardback)
Subjects: LCGFT: Poetry.
Classification: LCC PS3616.E8429 F64 2024 | DDC 811/.6—dc23/eng/20230713
LC record available at https://lccn.loc.gov/2023031243

Paperback ISBN: 978-0-374-61398-3

Designed by Crisis

Our books may be purchased in bulk for promotional, educational,
or business use. Please contact your local bookseller or the Macmillan
Corporate and Premium Sales Department at 1-800-221-7945, extension 5442,
or by email at MacmillanSpecialMarkets@macmillan.com.

www.fsgbooks.com
Follow us on social media at @fsgbooks

10 9 8 7 6 5 4 3 2 1

FOR WALT HUNTER

We dream of foreign countries, of other times and races of men, placing them at a distance in history or space; but let some significant event like the present occur in our midst, and we discover, often, this distance and this strangeness between us and our nearest neighbors. They are our Austrias, and Chinas, and South Sea Islands. Our crowded society becomes well spaced all at once, clean and handsome to the eye,—a city of magnificent distances. We discover why it was that we never got beyond compliments and surfaces with them before; we become aware of as many versts between us and them as there are between a wandering Tartar and a Chinese town. The thoughtful man becomes a hermit in the thoroughfares of the market-place. Impassable seas suddenly find their level between us, or dumb steppes stretch themselves out there. It is the difference of constitution, of intelligence, and faith, and not streams and mountains, that make the true and impassable boundaries between individuals and between states.

—HENRY DAVID THOREAU,

"A Plea for Captain John Brown"

CONTENTS

I

FOG

It never covered everything like a shroud.
It was always suspended over
like nineteenth-century women waiting for proposals.

It was an alphabet on top
of the one you knew, a redo,
trills on the scales, glissando.
It knew what it was doing between you.

It is very patient, teaching
you, it was different from the world, it waited
for you to say, *I do not understand.*

I was like everyone else.
I stopped lifting weights and walked
instead, I did not shop
if I could help it, found new use
for what I had.
I did inside what I had done
in the world. When I thought
about what I lost, I loved myself.

It comes from the ocean.
It means our interior burns.
Our coolness burns, miles inland.

It was haphazard.
It liked to see you altered
in your usual location.

It is admirable when it arrives
in the evening, it shadows the sunset.
We should challenge what's gone before.
The stories of heroes should almost
end several times before they end.

It was made of water, but not helpfully,
a stag walked inside. It was a voice
on the radio, a voice-over,
telling us about the technical difficulties
making the funeral hard to hear
at the moment when the great man's death
became a family matter.

A stag became concealed
at the moment a car turned the corner.
It required the driver
to do more than pay attention.
You have to be slow
in advance of what's coming.

The funeral came back with music.
A song about what could last.

It stayed the same, hanging
around the house

like a lovesick teenager
or a grown-up with nothing to do,
or curtains, or sirens, anything
with duration that acts permanent.

Milk spills across the kitchen
table with the children watching
in slow motion and the mother
watching the children in slow
motion, and she thinks, *I am the only*
one left, there is no one left
to wash the dishes or the children but me.

The fog comes home
through the Golden Gate, it has no home
in the ocean. What an absurd thought.

Highway paving itself,
making off-ramps as it goes,
bringing travelers of obscure
origin, but certain intention, steady.

It is as lofty as they come.

It touches everyone.

It's like God—it disappears.

It wants us to see ourselves.

Its absence is clear.

It didn't curtain the ocean. It curtained
the bay, the place the ocean
becomes domesticated, the name we give
to water land delays.

It sailed in on its own damn time
like a director looking for a star
and finding only waitresses and waitresses.
We auditioned for a year.

It sized us up as we stood still.
Our posture became
a version of the poet's gesture.
Attention turned into a question.

You can climb out of it.
I climbed the same hill every day
for a season, past the science
museum, and the place they split the atom.
The sense of accomplishment
became ordinary.

It was not arranged for your benefit.
Inside, you couldn't see in front of you.
Once above, you could only see a blank
covering what you usually knew.

On my walk, I wore our ethic
so everyone could see I was a person.
I created a tiny mist next to myself.
That was between me and the mask.
A basic nuisance, nothing special.
I didn't need to talk about it.

It falls into a category
defined by patterning
of language, a necessity to repeat:
experiences that feel like church but aren't.

I wish you would come back
is what we say to what
we love.
Also, *go away.*

Any return structures a day—
naked, my sister and I
greeted our father
dancing and laughing at the door.
We were almost too young to speak.
Did that ever happen?

Without you, I can't describe you,
I say to the fog,
you are different from people.
I can't keep space.

Though your cause
lifted you up, it did not release you.

Recantation of the ocean,
as faithful as possible for a variable
spirit, you're not like smoke, I can breathe you,
you can't take down a house.

I've been speaking about it at a distance.

Now I want to talk about its thickness.

A person could get killed in here.

I welcomed it the way
I welcomed love—not a lover, there wasn't
an agent, it was the change
I made, not the dollar
I broke to make it. Like money, power flows
to the people. When it leaves us, we riot.

Riot of droplets, organized
by expulsion. What can't be seen
clings to dust like a scholar
once said the soul did.
Fog's not the only body
stays numinous all its life.

It actually wanted to give you back to yourself.
I don't think it possessed one ounce of progress—
we saw ourselves in the same place
when it dispersed. The city took its usual

shape, buildings implying the streets
underneath that give them findable
addresses, places to deliver postal mail,
boxes in which letters could be dropped
through slots and sorted into people.

We could even see
how to get there again.
Rituals began in moderation.
Midmorning traffic like blood in a vein.

II

THE INTERIOR

A winter night in desert light:
trucks carving out air-corridors
of headlight on the interstate
at intervals only a vigil
could keep. Constellations
so clean you can see
the possibilities denied.

Now, from the beginning,
tell me everything.

THE TEACHER
AND THE STUDENT

At one time they could have been
lovers, one taking the train
fifteen minutes after the other
to not arouse suspicion, her black silk
skirt for Christmas left
hanging in the closet, the ivory
blouse with mother-of-pearl buttons
left with one unbuttoned on the
hanger, the pleated lace jabot
to warm the neck in church but also
for elegance, left on the dresser
whose top drawer held her mother's Psalter
and a fist-sized burlap satchel of lavender
scenting her camisole and stockings,
because her teacher, meeting
his students in seminar each day and even
Sunday afternoons if they were serious
enough about Augustine's *City of God* to translate

the text themselves with the aid of a dictionary
had already seen her in everything she owned,
his gaze glued now to a cardboard ticket.
He'd gone first, and did not imagine her
moving forward on the later wheels
of an older train that braked and squealed
through those fields she worked earlier
summers, and even kissed a farmhand for fun,
telling the boy she might be back,
the fields of wheat that looked to her
like letters of a bemused alphabet,
catching her breath inside them, wondering
what school would be like when it came,
as if he could forestall what would take place
between them, hunker it so deep
inside his person, the way they would sit
at once together on the bed, the sheet pulled tight
in the way of train station hotels,
in that town two towns north where no one
knew them, as no school existed there,
where not one person would think it strange
that older and younger could be aligned
by rings so new and cheaply made
they looked like they came from a Spring Fair
and hers on the wrong finger out of fear

she might offend some god she'd been convinced
to discount since her father died at thirty-five
from syphilis her mother would describe
as punishment but would not say from what.
Keeping to his half of the seat,
the ticket taking up both of his hands
like bread doled out in some orphanage,
the scene could live like iron in the earth,
hard in the senses, liquid underneath.
She reaches for his top button with both hands
as he remembers what she asked in French
on the first day they knew they would tell each other
their troubles, not just their interpretations.
How did the philosopher who built the Church
want us to talk about our hearts? The one who knew
why Adam and Eve covered
their genitals rather than their mouths,
their mouths, which had done all the sinning—
not out of any fear of God,
but since they couldn't face what they had done
without talking about it.

THE WALK TO THE ROAD, WHEN DINNER WAS OVER

"It's a strange image," he said, "and strange persons
you're telling of."

"They're like us," I said.

—Plato, *Republic*

Together we watched the stars
come out in their
inequality—Venus at the edge
of the valley and lower
than Mars, who, for a time, upstaged the moon.

I walk alongside the barbed wire, grateful
for what I can't control,
the alignment of your thoughts
with mine. It's delicate.

Men abandon women
for years, or socially, and do you think
women can't feel it?

But oh the sweetness of one
man overrides the rest and no
argument can undo it.

Do you know the soul doesn't
scatter, isn't a thing
that can be scattered?

The soul doesn't scatter
after death but goes wherever
it came from so it matters
when you die if you've tried
to have an imagination.

Most men say they would
give birth if they could.

When you are old, you say,
you'll go to your children
in their households
with tools, until you can't.

You're going further.
The place in the mind where memory
gets kept. Go if you need to.

One lamb escaped from
the slaughter, she's in the pen
with the whole summer, a whole
Sierra in her eyes at sunset.

It is not advice I give you
but the kind of blessing that comes
from the bewildered heart—if you want to walk
through a field of flowers
you must also walk at night.

The friends you lost, like bodies
buried, navigate the earth,
they're walking, or they're at a dinner
party and you are furthest
from their mind.

You can always look at the moon,
crescent moving
into Leo, and somehow
this is good for you?

You can do
things to the moon in the desert,
you can make it stand
still, you can make it move.

You climbed the mountain with me, a recovering
moralist. You wanted to stay
on the path, I wanted to find it.

November. Making a list
of people who can be trusted—
the one who said the owl's *who*
woke her up
from a dream of a winged horse.

I trusted the poet who wrote,
death is harder for the dying,
though it hurts the living more.

The place you imagine people go
when all of this is over, no one lies
there, no one misleads you
the way they do on earth.

I wanted to know how to behave
when the worst isn't over
but the best hasn't shown up yet.

I don't believe
the argument ended,
Try to be good versus *say what's true*

I'm standing in the dead center,
that place called the middle distance.
Taking the place of heaven,
the mountains we could die in
if we traveled without water.

Sound rustles through the ranch.

Don't blink. The beautiful
is sometimes the good. Don't get
excited. Not all the time.

They won't say thinking
was the only thing I did. I metabolized
what other people thought
into the facts of what they felt.

There's no one for miles.
That road leads
nowhere, into the mountains,
to an old mining claim
populated on paper, given a mayor,
used for a voting scam.

In the time of miracles, you could change
your mind by falling
off a horse. This isn't that time.

We could just become shapes
on a night like this, we could walk
into space and become clouds.

They will say to us, what
did you do in those days
to survive?
We married each other.

THE COUNTRY

A woman stands like a god in the field.
She moves a broken apparatus,
a wheeled line for irrigation, its length
expandable, but equal
to the length of what will hold a harvest
when it grows what we have
asked it to. We are alive together.
Everything that works has been repaired.
What hasn't, doesn't, and it doesn't matter.
A small engine sends water under pressure
into a metal channel that a handful
of arm's-length axles bound to shining circles
spin toward the sun. She makes them spin.
I wonder if she's tired of her anger.
Six flash floods closed our pass six times.
None of us got anything we needed.
This farm gets seven cuttings a year
of purple, luscious, drowsy alfalfa.
Don't ask a dream what order it was in.
Is being happy like not being hungry?

Show me a question that doesn't eat its answer.
How does it feel to work the land
in such dry heat, surrounded by coyotes?
The ones we live with are almost tame
and run among us, like they were our dogs,
entitled to a meal at the back door, or names.

WHAT DID PEOPLE
ASK OF EACH OTHER

on board ship,

sailing toward a war you didn't make,

or after that,

in the time of the athletes,

when we used games

to find out who was stronger,

or now, in the time

of the babies

crawling together

on a cotton mat

embroidered

with balloons, a numbered clock

and a large sun smiling

next to a sleeping moon,

spread out

in the middle of the room

to help them know

what time might be,

even before

they could learn

to tell it, and right this

minute when our

baby is about

to roll over and surprise

us with what we've made?

People asked each other to be brave.

THE SUPERMOON

starts the year off with so much light
it wakes everyone up. Its whiteness
disquiets. It does not shine a beam.
In January, life's not as it seems—
it's flat. I had my child like that,
cesarean. Caesar,
the general who fell. But the day
his friends knifed him he threw his toga
on like all was well. My daughter's swaddle
declines into a toga. The way it shimmies
in the morning shows how she slept.
Morning, when dreams get erased.
My daughter hates it when I leave the room.
People think Emily got her name
from poetry, but her Korean father chose it
so his family could say it without trouble.
Trouble, such a beautiful word,
I wish we would say it with abandon.
Once I thought we all agreed on kindness.
Then I ripped a spiderweb

because of some unmanageable fear.
There's no place for chopsticks
in an American drawer, my husband said.
I said, just try me. Just watch me try.
I'm American. I can put things anywhere.

SECOND FAMILY

I lived on a farm. It was my second family.
It was also a school that educated men
to become servants to humanity.
I talked about it like it was my home.

Between the wars, Freud writes to his friend, he does not
believe in God but recognizes
others have experienced an oceanic feeling,
a fantasy of life within the womb.

An animal once told me how to feel,
a black and white member of my second family.
She dropped a wet calf on my birthday
walking away as it called for her.

I loved the womb more when I had to use it.
Sitting at the teaching table
at the school where my second family lived,
my girl kicked me while I lectured.

The middle child of a firstborn mother,
I lived as other without black sheep power,
on the lookout for a different order
since the first Christmas I moved lambs to the manger.

Everyone should learn to feed the animals.
The object was to farm a piece of desert,
growing food out of necessity.
No Swiss-made sweet milk. Ours tasted like sage.

Young men covered in sour milk from mornings
early in the dairy, no time for laundry,
arguing against the oceanic feeling,
and there I was, a Russian doll, a matryoshka,

I saw inside her another family,
another, and another, and another,
and so on, like a repeating decimal.
The more we talked, the more the baby kicked.

Where is your home, where are you going, I see you are like
    me,
stranded, buoyed only a little, only a decimal's worth,
by that perishable angel, the passage of time, who does not
    discriminate,

I said to my girl, who could not hear words yet,

just sounds, with the voice you use when you are talking
    silently,
within a family, a country, a world
to someone you already love.
I learned this voice from my second family.

Julian made a speech about the wind
Abram cooked masterpieces for children
Alexander double-dug the garden beds
Justin built a cabin with no walls

STARS, DAYS, WORDS

We call days what nights leave behind.
My daughter points out the stars to me
(she is sitting on her father's shoulders)
as if I had not seen them before she came
and might have missed them except for her eyes.
You don't need to go far to see the world.
She has words and a sentence or two.
You tell me what's going fast as this.

THE NIGHT

No one knows when the night begins.
There must be a moment, no
one has learned it yet, even the baby
knows that it exists, she asks,
is it getting dark, and we say yes,
just before it becomes time to eat.

*

We all study the sunset,
we look and tell each other to look.
Our view through trees stays free
and close, lucky, we do not have
to pay or drive to keep
ourselves aligned with time
by looking at what looks like fire,
staying a little longer without burning.

*

No one knows when the night begins
if beginning means preparing for sleep—first the fairies
chase the children across the little plate.
The baby's left hand forks her bite of chicken,
a gesture centered in the wrist, like a first letter,
in this case, an E a bit like a weathervane.
The fairies chase the children's green wheelbarrow
as bits of salt and fat get taken
off the surface by the water in the washer
and go into the ground, and they continue
to chase the children's faces in a story
we cannot seem to find in any of our books.

*

Someone is always putting the baby to bed.
The baby loves the book about the storm
and says so, loves the mother
rocking the baby in the storm book
who resembles a bundle
of clothes a runaway might assemble
and says so, says, I love that page, says,
I want that page to be the ending.

*

Everyone understands the moment
the lights go off does not equal the moment sleep
begins but has anyone discovered whether
this could be the beginning of the night?
Many have rearranged both
comforter and pillow to deliberate the point.
The raccoon mothers have never asked.
Night persists in the noses of the deer.

    *

The daughter goes to sleep in her room
with one parent, and we call this
going down with the ship.
The other has moved on from poetry
to news. This leads to commentary
on events of the day, opinions.
Children belong in school.
People cannot agree on that.

    *

The one who does not read stays
until the baby sleeps, until the child
says, Quiet Time, until the child turns

her face to the wall and snores.
Is this the moment the night begins?
Is this moment the icy measure
of the three of them entering
into nature and the conditions
of necessity together?

*

Mother or father in the room with the child,
mother or father sleeping under a book.
Some nights a parent falls asleep with the child,
some nights two parents fall asleep together.
None of these is a final arrangement,
simply the end of the beginning, tender
as apology after anger.
Moonlight turns the beds into glaciers.

THE FIRE MAP

Their symbols are single flames. Every fire
requires a pretty name—Apple, Blue Jay, Coyote.
They earned those names by starting where they did.
And you can find them if you pause the arrow
on the map, and press with your finger, but not too hard.
If you do that, you'll be sent back
to the first map, laid out in its bordered shape,
the template of the state.

That isn't what you wanted to see.
But once there, you can advance,
investigating fires from previous years, whose symbols are
    the same,
placed differently, on identical maps, since the terrain
hasn't changed its surface, though the water table
would tell a different story. Paradise and its shotgun canyons
a few years back, a fire in Trinity the previous that turned
    into a complex
(they call a fire a complex when it grows)
merging with the blaze that began

in lava beds. That perimeter
included nearly half of a national monument.
But—see!—you can no longer find those names.

Last decade's Rim Fire simply reads "contained." The symbols
turn red the year we're in. They gray them
for each year that's gone before. The current map
changes with the hour, look, the Sheep Fire
just showed up on the shadowed topography near Lassen,
where two years ago another fire raged,
south of Susanville, town named for a miner's daughter,
which didn't have a post office or bank
until three years after its name became official,
or so they teach you in school. The map says it's just 3 percent
    contained.
But like all numbers, these mislead,
as success isn't about amount for those who fight
but some cessation of agility—if the fire can jump,
can they keep up? A fire can burn contained
much longer than it does what it came to do.
Under these symbols, the map of California wrinkles

like a sheet on a sad bed, easy to fix, but hard to make right
when one remains preoccupied with troubles,
as the relationship that happened there caused you

to abandon the basics of care,

and has assumed a quality of being impossible

to end or heal, since getting out

means leaving for good, so you wonder,

will you be followed

for years by all you've said

and done? They colored the map

where the land deserved it. The desert shouldn't claim

everything the eye can see from space. Doesn't water

deserve a better color than white? But just as many flames
    live there,

in the green spaces, where mountains hold and give

the snowpack that diminishes each year—

red in the present tense, they are nearly festive, like lights
    on trees.

Incidents on the wane turn a darker green.

The map disappears five years after they make it.

Twelve years ago was awful—

now it's gone. You'd have to talk to someone

who lived through those fires to find out what burned.

In no year does this map record our smoke.

ARGUMENT
WITH A CHILD

If you don't do this thing you can't
do the next thing and I know
you want to do the next thing.

How do I know?
I'll tell you when I'm older.
Look at the flowers.

Can you say wisteria.
You don't want to say wisteria.
You'd rather die is the look on your face.

How can I fix it if you won't
let me look at it?
Look at something else while I touch it.

Plant your eyes on that place mat of the world
you love and don't
move them until it stops hurting.

THE ALPHABET, FOR EMILY

In your picture book of letters,
the B obscures a bee.
You are interested in this.
My memory of language begins later.

I was supposed to remember words
and put them on a page, the next morning
as they were called out by my teacher.
I was discovering the patterns when I got lost

watching my mother fold the laundry.
I was imagining a line across my room
and on one side, hoopskirted ladies
rode in carriages, and on the other, in the present tense,

nothing could be beautiful.
I was watching the rain order
the rosebush, *surrender your petals*.
Or I got lost fighting with my sister.

*

You like anything with a problem.
A country could learn from this and love

itself more, with all its nicks and scratches.
I am afraid of giving you too much credit.

Truth's pressure on a mother
terrifies as much as a monster.

When a child loves the alphabet
there's nothing moral about it.

*

It was in the nature of, it was fundamental
to the alphabet that a person could be wrong.
It was buried deep in the activity,
like the idea of virginity.

*

I tried so hard to repeat and remember
but I wanted to go forward in the book.
You go forward as quickly as I
remember wanting to, burning

through your picture books and workbooks
so frustrated you can't learn

the way you eat your dinner—
you look at that, it disappears,
you destroy your obligation to it,
sleepy as it turns into your fuel.

      *

They asked me to remember the rules.
But I could only memorize for pleasure.
Cake and all the words that rhymed—delicious.
And you could try out any sound in your head.

Language means you don't have to learn
in front of other people.

C on the next page moves the problem
along—what it starts with isn't what it is.
It conceals warships, hides sunken jewelry.
Unfathomable to us, the sea is rising.

THE MOTHER

Watching a good father with his daughter
can heal a person, it is like water, to see
them together on the beach with a yellow bucket
between them and she digs

a hole big enough to bury his feet
up to the ankles and leave him smiling
to stay where she puts him, even
pulling out his phone to take a picture

of her running away toward the changing
margin of the lake, testing
whether he could get out and grab
her if she stumbled in the water, whether

his feet have been truly trapped
by her decisions or whether her seriousness
can't yet do to sand what she has done of late
to sentences: exactly what she wants.

Watching her refute the water
with ankles I believe mine still resemble
I think into the stories I can't tell her
about the summer I spent in a state

I never returned to with a man
who didn't think the wildfires
should keep us from pleasure.
Years before, my father

wished he never taught me to take pictures
since he felt my sunsets imprecise,
telling me, just take the people out.
At least what I can't tell her now.

I am so good at watching the earth.
My judgment comes in secret. It remains as fair
as nature, and nature is the force
that makes all seasons end when they should.

SMOKE

Dylan came by and we sat unmasked.
We had seen enough of each other all summer
we were almost quarantining together,
and he'd been tested twice in the last month
but afterward I took a shower and cried.
Phyllis didn't go for a walk, her lungs
are ninety, she's not an idiot, but her daughter
Pacia did, Pacia once took pictures
of clandestine midwives in the sixties
illegally watching over the births of children.
They kept our children inside
before lunch, but after that the air seemed fine
though Luna's mother said she coughed at night
and Paloma herself, all of two,
told me at pickup she smelled like camping.
Margaret said it wasn't so bad yesterday
in the Central Valley where it is generally much
worse but today it was no good and she was crying
not feeling-tears but the other kind,
the kind your body makes when it's wise.

Young and Emily are fine, thank you for writing
to ask me about them, dead mother, I have heard
the whole world is now getting letters
from the dead, actual letters, addressed to them,
in human envelopes, with stamps of American rivers,
delivered through the mail. Since the Post Office
is about to die, the land of the dead, its government,
have decided for now to take it over,
that they could do a better job than we could.
And I agree. The letter I received
from you, written in a splendid hand
on pink paper with a deckle edge,
looked just like the year that you were born,
when warships docked in San Francisco Bay
and ordinary city blocks had wardens
and margarine was what you ate on bread.
And since we cannot send a letter back
because your invisible address
flummoxes our advanced forensics
I will write this and burn it in a bowl
secretly inside my house since there are city
rules about flames at a time like this.
If you won't be reached by words, by smoke
my love will reach you with our story.

FAMILY

All I knew was that I would not let them die
alone, the images, the image of the father
with his daughter pulled into his shirt, her head
tucked into his armpit like a lamb
in a description of a shepherd in a novel
by Thomas Hardy, arms around each other
so they would not be separated
if they drowned, but then they drowned.

THE WEB

Never seen a whole
one until now—
not one broken
line, connections
flawless. Unfrayed.
From this angle,
below the hedge
that borders my neighbor
looking toward
the upslope of the ordinary
driveway, that border
orients my sight
to the right, and sunlight
makes the spinning
visible, light
leaning on one line,
then another,
shining between
the elements
until the filament

moves just
a bit, and all
of the strands shine
visible, each,
in turn, more visible
so the last moves
more than a person
thinks it could
in the actual wind, making
the whole web
move, though you do
not need such
assurance, such
a view, to be reminded
that the web has
been fashioned to spread
across the hedge
since the maker, her mottled
abdomen, splendid
as a ceramic intended
to be beautiful for daily use,
situated in the middle,
extends her legs and arms
to say, I made this. But seen,
or rather, squinted

toward from the other
angle, from the top
of the poured
asphalt whose fierce
downslope
makes the emergency
brake feel
insufficient for
the car you park,
the same web
suspended between
the hedge
and an offshoot
of the hedge, from this
vantage closer
to the street, here,
only by the maker
can her web be seen,
her body just
as visible, her health
thrown into relief
by her invisible
work. I wanted
to see from both
sides what she spun

last night before
she ate. She is not
going anywhere
if she can help it.
I am trying to put
the child in the car.
The child goes to play
as I go to work.
There is only ever
enough space
to open the door
and get barely in.
Do I try to not
disturb the maker
from the angle
where I can see
her and what she
has made, opening
the car door gingerly
and moving
around its side with
the child, who certainly
will resist the stillness
such a task asks
of her, with

what I am trying
not to destroy
all the time visible?
Or do I walk around
the side of the car
and open the door
intuitively,
the way I do every
morning, toward
me, without being
able to see
the spider or her web?
Let us preserve what we can.
Desire brings the child
and the spider
together, it's like a house
that's crowded
but not ever full.
I remember the tension
in the web, the focused
light, the way the spider
sat on top
of what she ate,
pairing one art with
a darker art,

killing exactly what
you need to live,
no more than that.
Sorry for your
trouble, the Irish
say to each other
after death walks in.
The wake's a party.
Everyone shows up.
I look. I see I haven't
wrecked her.
I buckle my daughter.

AMERICANS

He lost his job. He didn't know what to say
to his family so he sat in the train station all afternoon
and told each person waiting a different story.
She made a quilt for her baby. She had to sell it for money
and since it worked the first time, she did it again.
Now she sells everything she makes to other people.
He didn't have enough to bring his parents over
so they died in a place where he could never visit them.
He had to marry her to keep her here.
Rain, snow on the monument to the boats
that settled the fishing town on the northern spit
in a state most of us will never visit.
More snow on that pass where people died
when they had had to eat pine branches, then each other.
Enough wind to make the government warn us.
She grew up on that land but never owned it.
He owned it years ago and lost it in a game.
She didn't grow up here but she planted
poppies, wild iris, sun cups, lupines. Those native
plants you see, she planted them all,

seeds she ordered from another state.

She had an idea the soil could be reminded,

not that soil has ever lived for pleasure,

she thought she could make an agreement with it.

He couldn't help his children with their homework.

She never had children, only ideas.

Together the two of them built this house,

and together let it rot in rain and weather.

Were they taking their loneliness out on each other?

Did they simply not understand abundance,

the way in which it asks you to quit asking?

He loved his partner's dogs more than his partner,

and they were very beautiful, who could blame him,

a silver gray sheepdog and a spotted heeler.

It made her so mad when he went to that church,

she quit getting up in the morning.

She decided that her world should just be night.

When they were in public, he said, *only speak English*.

The boats they used to own ended up firewood.

What beautiful fires our houses made that winter.

THE DEER IN FIRE SEASON

It isn't love that makes them
come nestle each other under
the liquid amber after they eat
all the ivy, dahlias and the stock.
The doe only half naps,
eyes half-open, trained
on threats. She fogs her sight
to resemble its lack, convincing
others she doesn't pay
attention, the exact way I endure
regrets (smoke-screening
deeper fears). Neither is the cause
of their loyalty to this location
fear, nor is it hunger.
It is nothing particular to our plot.
Husband, you should not be surprised.
I have seen you as particular
at a restaurant early in our caring

for each other, choosy
over a table in the sun. I live
with your distastes—cilantro, small talk,
slapstick. I appreciate
what you tolerate—humiliation on the human
level, sleepless nights. I know how immovable you are.
So chase the mother with your camera—it is you
who instructed me the leisure
of animals finds equivalence
only in art. See, she lets her children
escape first. She wants to stall us,
so let us be still
humans who can lose track
of time. Watch her leg, it's like a lower limb
of eucalyptus, pushing winter.
It looks like tinder.

THE BEACH

No one could prohibit the sunshine.
All the churches were shut.
Families headed to the water.

Little fear, rest, I said to my child,
the waves crash too far out to be interested
in you. Keep on with your story in the sand.

You live with mama in a cave.
Shells are food this holiday.
Bundle feathers to burn so we won't freeze.

Fire is a resource that can't be saved.

NOTES

THE TEACHER AND THE STUDENT

This poem freely imagines a relationship similar to the one between the philosophers Hannah Arendt and Martin Heidegger, using details from Elisabeth Young-Bruehl's biography of Arendt, *Hannah Arendt: For Love of the World*, and incorporating other elements of my own design.

THE WALK TO THE ROAD, WHEN DINNER WAS OVER

The epigraph misquotes Allan Bloom's inimitable translation of Plato's *Republic*. It is from Book VII, the well-known Allegory of the Cave. I began writing this poem in 2016, when I was teaching the *Republic*. At some point during the process of composition, I wrote down these lines from memory, placing them inside an earlier version of the poem. The words established themselves, as written down, with conviction. As the poem persisted, my incorrect quotation of Bloom's translation persisted as well. The Greek lines are as follows:

Ἄτοπον, ἔφη, λέγεις εἰκόνα καὶ δεσμώτας ἀτόπους.
Ὁμοίους ἡμῖν, ἦν δ᾽ ἐγώ.

And Bloom's rendering is:

> "It's a strange image," he said, "and strange prisoners you're telling of."
>
> "They're like us," I said.

My error is too much a part of my poem now for me to change it back.

THE NIGHT

The Storm Book by Charlotte Zolotow (Harper & Brothers, 1952).
This poem is for Margaret Ronda and Claire Waters.

THE FIRE MAP

www.fire.ca.gov/incidents.
"More delicate than the historians' are the map-makers' colors."
—Elizabeth Bishop, "The Map"

ACKNOWLEDGMENTS

Grateful acknowledgment is given to the editors of the following publications, in which some of these poems previously appeared or will appear, sometimes in slightly different form: *The Atlantic, Changes Review, The Cortland Review, Harvard Review, Literary Imagination, Literary Matters, Los Angeles Review of Books, The Nation, The New York Review of Books, Poem-a-Day, Poetry London, Poetry Northwest, Santa Clara Review, The Yale Review.*

"The Web" received the Meringoff Poetry Award from the Association of Literary Scholars, Critics, and Writers in 2020.

I thank the Chancellor's Club Fund at the University of California, Davis, and the Foundation for Contemporary Arts, for generous support during the years in which this book was written.

Thanks to my friends with keen eyes and ears who read these poems in draft.